Original title:
Petals of Eden

Copyright © 2025 Creative Arts Management OÜ
All rights reserved.

Author: Dorian Ashford
ISBN HARDBACK: 978-1-80566-757-5
ISBN PAPERBACK: 978-1-80566-827-5

Blossoms in a Sunlit Reverie

In the garden, flowers dance,
Wearing hats made of grass,
Bees are buzzing like a band,
Trying hard not to crash.

Daisies gossip 'bout the breeze,
Casting quirks with every sway,
Tulips laugh, they're such a tease,
Wishing for a holiday.

Sunflowers wear their sunny smiles,
Counting clouds like sheep at night,
Chasing shadows, playing styles,
In a game that feels just right.

Ladybugs in polka dots,
Doing cha-cha on the lawn,
While the snails take timid shots,
Dropping trails and then they're gone.

With each bloom, a giggle flows,
Nature's party never ends,
In this realm where laughter grows,
Life's a joke that never bends.

Nature's Kiss on Bare Skin

Sunshine tickles toes and feet,
Dancing grass beneath the beat.
Bees buzzing like a tiny band,
Nature's mischief, oh so grand!

A butterfly steals my muffin,
I chase it down, we're really bluffin'.
Squirrels giggle from the trees,
While I tumble, oh dear me!

Symphony of Color and Light

Crayons melted in the sun,
Rainbows burst, oh what a fun!
A purple cow in the meadow prances,
While daffodils join in silly dances.

The bluebirds sing off-key each morn,
While flowers make the bees feel worn.
Nature's palette spills and splashes,
Giggles echo, the humor crashes.

The Hidden Oasis

In the jungle, I seek a drink,
But find a cow that loves to wink.
Palm trees sway with mischievous glee,
As monkeys steal my K.O. tea!

Coconuts drop, a plop then crash,
I duck just in time, oh what a splash!
A lizard laughs, then gives a grin,
In this oasis, I can't help but spin.

Juxtaposition of Shadows and Shades

A funky shadow at my feet,
Dancing wildly to a beat.
The sun plays tricks, oh what a scene,
As grasshoppers act like they're on a screen.

Whimsical shapes in the evening light,
A cat pretends it's ready for a fight.
But then it naps in the sun's warm glow,
While I'm left to watch this funny show!

Wings of the Flowering Spirit

In a garden where daisies dance,
Bees wear tiny pants,
They buzz with glee, quite silly indeed,
What a humorous stance!

Tulips gossip in the breeze,
Sharing secrets with the bees,
Their petals flutter, like a fan,
In this wacky flower spree!

Lilies laugh at the sun's bright beam,
Jumping high on a brilliant gleam,
Their roots take a goofy leap,
In this botanical dream!

Morning glories giggle at dawn,
Spreading smiles on the lawn,
With colors that tickle the eye,
It's nature's way to yawn!

Shades of Nature's Reverie

In a forest, trees wear capes,
Joking with the silly shapes,
Squirrels in sunglasses prance around,
Dodging their leafy drapes!

A wise old owl hoots with flair,
Cracking jokes without a care,
While the flowers chuckle softly,
In this whimsical lair!

Mossy rocks join in the fun,
Playing tag with the setting sun,
Each shadow skips and dances,
Until the day is done!

A breeze tickles blades of grass,
Making whispers that amass,
Nature's laughter all around,
In a delightful, green mass!

The Breath of the Garden

In a patch where veggies chat,
Tomatoes in a baseball hat,
They dream of games beneath the sun,
But they can't run, imagine that!

Carrots join a waltz so grand,
With radishes, they take a stand,
The lettuce spins, it's quite a sight,
In this dance-filled band!

Herbs tell tales of savory nights,
While beans aim for silly heights,
Chasing clouds as they float by,
In whimsical delights!

At dusk, the garden sighs with glee,
Winking at the moonlit sea,
For in this plot of jovial bliss,
Laughter is the key!

Reverent Roots of Time

In the soil, where wisdom's found,
Roots giggle under the ground,
They curl and twist with laughter shared,
In this earthy playground!

A tortoise hums a slow refrain,
While clouds above start to complain,
"Why so rushed? Just slow your flow!"
"You've much to gain, my friend, it's plain!"

Beneath the stars, old tales unfold,
Of daring blooms and roots so bold,
In this sleepy, funny world,
Where time's more precious than gold!

As crickets sing their funny tunes,
The garden smiles at the glowing moons,
For in this realm of giggles bright,
Nature's joy forever looms!

A Mosaic of Life

In the garden of giggles, flowers chat,
Bees wear tiny hats, how about that?
A snail races past, it's quite a sight,
It won a gold medal in the slowest fight.

Roses tell secrets, oh what a tease,
While daisies dance on a gentle breeze.
That old oak tree tells jokes all day,
While the sun chuckles in its golden ray.

Every bloom has a story, a joke to unfold,
Like the shy gardenia, too bashful and bold.
They say laughter is the best form of cheer,
So let's plant some smiles, my friend, never fear!

In this patchwork of joy, let nature play,
With whimsical blooms that brighten the day.
Each color and fragrance, a humorous twist,
In the comedy show, come laugh and assist!

Luminous Gossamer Trails

In twilight whispers, fireflies gleam,
Wobbling like jellybeans in a dream.
A spider spins webs of glitter and trails,
As crickets recount their grandest tales.

Funny hats on every daffodil's head,
They gossip about the bugs in their bed.
Shimmering shadows, quite the parade,
As stars poke fun at the moon's charade.

Wandering thoughts on petals so bright,
Comedians rustle through the night.
Who knew that blooms could have such flair?
A giggling garden is beyond compare!

With laughter mixed in the evening air,
The flowers giggle without a care.
In this playful realm of gossamer light,
Every turn brings a chuckle, pure delight!

Scent of the Scribbled Cosmos

In a universe scribbled with colors and scents,
The flowers hold court, making goofy intents.
A jester tulip trips over a bee,
While lilies roll laughter, oh what glee!

A daffodil whispers sweet gossip at night,
Under starlit giggles, a merry sight.
Sunflowers wear shades, looking so cool,
While the fencepost debates if it's a stool.

Comets of daisies zip through the sky,
With petals like krispy treats, oh my!
The scent of silly fills the whole town,
Even grumpy old rocks start laughing, no frown.

This cosmos of humor, blooming and bright,
Where even the weeds join in on the light.
With every inhale, joy floats on by,
In this garden of laughter, let's reach for the sky!

The Poetry of New Growth

Every sprout is a poet, bold and spry,
Telling tales of the sun and the rain up high.
With roots in the soil, they dance and they sway,
Making puns with the breeze, in clever play.

A baby fern flirts with the buzzing bees,
Offering riddles in the tickling breeze.
Petunias chuckle, with colors so bright,
Creating a scene that's pure delight.

New buds share dreams with the glittering dew,
Spinning with laughter, there's so much to do.
In this lively chorus, blooms twist and twirl,
Transforming it all into a giggly whirl.

So let's celebrate growth with a chuckle and cheer,
In this garden of humor where smiles appear.
Nature's funny poem, forever unfurled,
In this joyful spectacle, oh what a world!

Vibrations of the Verdant Vale

In the vale where daisies dance,
Squirrels pull their shiny prance.
A rabbit wearing a top hat,
Is quite the sight, imagine that!

The bees hold buzzing concerts loud,
While frogs form quite the jumping crowd.
A tortoise claims the title of king,
Saying, "Slow and steady's my best thing!"

When flowers giggle in the breeze,
Sunshine winks, oh such tease!
Even the clouds can't help but grin,
Watching this grand show begin!

So if you wander through this place,
Join the fun at your own pace.
With laughter sprouting all around,
Find joy where silly vibes abound!

The Blooming Tranquility

In the garden, blooms wear hats,
Butterflies laugh with chitchat.
The daisies gossip, what a scene,
Saying, "Have you seen that bee?"

A sunflower's towered crown so proud,
Bows to the tulips from the crowd.
A gnome with mischief in his eyes,
Whispers to a worm, "Let's start a prize!"

Daffodils show off their dance moves,
While grasshoppers groove in their grooves.
Every petal's a party, so come!
Join the fun, don't feel glum!

Nature's chuckles fill the air,
In this realm without a care.
So let your spirit lift and sing,
For joy is what these flowers bring!

Soulful Springs of Life

At spring's door, the laughter flows,
With tulips tickling tiny toes.
A daffodil dances, oh so bright,
Curtsying to the morning light.

The pond's a stage for frogs to croak,
With jokes that make the lilies choke.
A mouse tries surfing on a leaf,
While a snail explains, "No need for grief!"

A wily wind, it swirls and spins,
Knocking hats off hedgehogs' chins.
The air's alive with giggles and glee,
As buds burst forth for all to see!

So when you see blooms in delight,
Join their fun from dawn till night.
For in this patch, life's never rough,
Every petal sings, "Life is enough!"

A Caress from the Flora

With petals soft, the blossoms play,
Tickling bees throughout the day.
A leafy friend's a jolly sight,
Trying to dance with all its might!

Violets giggle, what a craze,
As they blush in the sun's warm rays.
A wandering ant hums a tune,
While daisies sway beneath the moon.

Cactus tries its aim at humor,
But pokes out wise, "I'm just a bloomer!"
In gardens where the colors burst,
Giggling blooms quench joy and thirst!

So when you wander through the green,
Let laughter fill spaces unseen.
For every leaf and petal's cheer,
Brings whimsy to this atmosphere!

Orchard of Reveries

In a grove where dreams reside,
Apples giggle, peaches slide.
Cherries chat about the sun,
While bananas just want to run.

Squirrels boast of acorn finds,
While bees hum silly rhymes.
A watermelon wore a tie,
And danced beneath the blue sky.

Plums play poker on the grass,
Lemons shout, "Come on, you lass!"
Limes do flips, they're quite the show,
The orchard's laughter starts to grow.

As twilight brings a chillier tease,
Cacti join, saying, "Oh, please!"
In this grove, joy's never far,
Just watch out for that dancing jar!

Dance of the Morning Dew

Plants are laughing in their beds,
Dewdrops bouncing on their heads.
Each leaf sways, trying to groove,
While sunlight starts its daily move.

Ladybugs are holding hands,
Sharing secrets of their lands.
The daisies tell a joke or two,
"Oh, who knew we'd dance this dew?"

Morning glory, a quirky bunch,
Spilling nectar in a crunch.
While a snail tries to steal the show,
"Just a minute, I'm moving slow!"

As the sun begins to climb,
Flowers twirl in perfect rhyme.
Sunday's best, and then some more,
A garden party—who could ask for more?

Serenade of Vibrant Hues

In a canvas where blooms collide,
Colors chat, they do not hide.
Bluebells sing the blues so sweet,
While violets tap their little feet.

Roses gossip, tales of flair,
"There's a bug, but who can care?"
Sunflowers stand tall, huge and bright,
Telling stories of their height.

Orchids flaunt their fancy frills,
While daisies drop some silly gills.
A daffodil pulls off a stunt,
And pansies giggle with a grunt.

As twilight drapes its silky cloak,
The garden laughs, what a joke!
In this place of splendid view,
Every shade knows how to woo.

Tides of Grace and Growth

Waves of green and blooms in sync,
Every bud has time to think.
A dandelion whispers soft,
"How'd I end up at this loft?"

Lilies float, as frogs sing loud,
In a pond, they draw a crowd.
All the critters join the fun,
"Join us now, or you're outdone!"

Butterflies burst into a race,
While grasses giggle with grace.
Tall reeds sway, a friendly tease,
"Who knew growing could be such a breeze?"

As the moon begins to rise,
Stars waltz down from velvet skies.
In the garden, all is bright,
Life's a game—what a delight!

Bridges Built by Blossoms

In a garden of giggles, flowers dance,
With wobbling bees that love to prance.
Petunias tease and violets grin,
Nectar sippers know where to begin.

Lilies in tutus twirl with delight,
While daisies wear glasses, silly in sight.
The sunflowers chuckle at the ants' parade,
While butterflies join in, unafraid.

A dandelion sneezes, puffs all around,
Making wishes fly high without making a sound.
The tulips throw a party, oh what a sight,
Where every bloom laughs through day and night.

In this colorful circus, joy is the norm,
Petals gossip lightly, and chaos can swarm.
Laughter takes root, in this playful spree,
Where flowers unite in floral jubilee.

Tides of the Floral Sea

Waves of blossoms crash on sandy shores,
With parrot tulips ready to explore.
Nasturtiums surf on petals so bright,
And zinnias laugh at the silly kite flight.

Roses wear caps, looking quite dapper,
While pansies whisper jokes, oh what a caper!
The ocean of color sways left and right,
As bees form a choir to sing through the night.

A crab strolls by in a floral disguise,
With sun-kissed geraniums making him rise.
The seaweed's a party, it's quite the affair,
Flowers enjoy the breeze in the salty air.

Seashells become vessels for the blooms to ride,
Floating along with their floral pride.
In this silly ocean, with waves made of cheer,
Laughter is plentiful, bringing all near.

Beneath the Awakened Canopy

Under the trees where mischief does dwell,
Fruits fall like jokes that are hard to tell.
Squirrels wear caps, and the raccoons smile,
As they frolic and dance in humorous style.

The sunlight filters through leaves like confetti,
While laughter spills out, all warm and heavy.
A butterfly barista serves nectar with flair,
To blooms that giggle in the fragrant air.

An acorn plays sax in a woodland band,
While daisies shake maracas with leaves in hand.
The undergrowth chuckles at every footfall,
As shadows play tag, in a leafy ball.

In this wooded kingdom where fun never ends,
The shrubs share secrets and giggle with friends.
Every shade and hue revels in delight,
Under the canopy, all feels just right.

Reflections in a Dewdrop

A dewdrop giggles on a leaf so proud,
Holding reflections of a boisterous crowd.
Daisies flip their hair, while crocuses yawn,
As the sun peeks in on this rosy dawn.

Ants wear top hats and march in a line,
While ladybugs chatter, sipping on wine.
In the glistening droplet, secrets are stored,
Of humorous tales from the daily hoard.

The raindrops join in with a tap-tap dance,
As mossy floor mats get their chance to prance.
In this little world, where laughter's the key,
All blooms gather round for a comedy spree.

With each tiny shimmer, joy finds its way,
In nature's vastness, the blooms like to play.
Reflections unite in a giggly parade,
Creating a symphony that never will fade.

Shadows of Blooming Night

In the garden, shadows play,
Plants are dancing, come what may.
A gnome is telling jokes, oh dear,
His laughter echoed, drink your beer!

Fireflies twinkle, light the way,
A cat joins in, on this fine day.
Chasing bugs, he makes a fuss,
Falling over, oh what a rush!

The Sentinels of Spring

The flowers gossip, what a sight,
Tulips whisper, big and bright.
A bee buzzes, "I'm the king!"
Makes the daisies laugh and sing.

The sun peeks through, a warming glow,
Squirrels try ballet, steal the show.
Oh, what chaos, plants in a swirl,
Mother Nature's playful twirl!

A Journey through Blossoming Paths

On this path, the blooms collide,
Pansies gossip, "Where's your pride?"
A snail slides by, all in a trance,
Takes a selfie, missed his chance!

Butterflies flit, with a flair,
Sharing secrets in the air.
A toad croaks out a silly tune,
Bopping along like he's the moon!

The Lullaby of Greenery

Under the leaves, whispers unfold,
Chlorophyll tales, eager and bold.
A raccoon juggles, trying to fit,
Trip over roots, what a hit!

The crickets chirp a night-time song,
While owls hoot, "We can't go wrong!"
A dance-off starts, stars twinkle bright,
In the greenery, all feels right!

Stillness Among the Fronds

Beneath the leaves, a rabbit sleeps,
While dreaming of the carrots he keeps.
A turtle confused, wearing a hat,
Says, "Why rush? I'm fine just like that."

The birds are gossiping on the vine,
"Did you hear? The sky's back on the line!"
A butterfly flirts, quite out of place,
While a snail just hopes for some space.

A frog croaks loud to get some attention,
But behind him, the flowers start a convention.
"Let's dance!" they cry, twirling with glee,
While the frog just sighs, "Why can't they see?"

In stillness found among the fronds,
Even the goofy moments respond.
The world can be silly, that much is true,
Just take a break, find your joy anew.

Heartbeats of the Ornate Orchid

In a garden where laughter blooms bright,
An orchid declares, "I'm ready for flight!"
It flaps its petals, a comical sight,
While bees nearby just wish it was night.

A ladybug rolls, claiming it's art,
Saying, "This dance? It won't break my heart!"
While a proud bumblebee starts a debate,
"I can buzz louder, just wait, just wait!"

A worm in the soil cultivates dreams,
"Have you heard about the vegetable teams?"
While daisies snicker, heads held up high,
"Don't you know? Roots like to lie!"

In the laughter of leaves, humor provides,
Simple heartbeats where joy resides.
So come join the fun, don't miss your cue,
In floral antics, there's always something new!

The Enchanted Arboretum

Among the trees, a squirrel makes plans,
To steal a snack from clumsy young hands.
With acorns stacked, he feels like a king,
While other critters around him just sing.

A wise owl yawns, full of complaints,
"Is this tree too tall for my ancient taints?"
While raccoons argue over who's a snack,
One claims, "I'm too tough to eat, cut me slack!"

A fox in disguise wears a floral crown,
Says, "I'm fashionable; time to sit down!"
While vines twist together, a gossiping crew,
"Did you hear? He's gone nuts, it's totally true!"

In this arboretum, mischief abounds,
With laughter and joy that knows no bounds.
So take a stroll, and lose all your care,
Nature's humor is just waiting to share!

Luminescence in the Meadow

In the meadow where candles light dreams,
A firefly dances, or so it seems.
It trips on blades, and giggles a tune,
"Oops! How'd I end up here at noon?"

A grasshopper jumps with a bounce and a sway,
"Hey, check out my moves! It's a sunny ballet!"
While daisies chuckle, their heads in the air,
"Look at that fool, he hasn't a care!"

An ant drags a crumb, it's bigger than him,
While the crowd starts cheering, encouraging him.
"Go, little buddy! You've got this for sure,"
As a butterfly joins with a laugh and a tour.

In this luminous field where friendships grow,
Every stumble becomes part of the show.
So laugh and be merry, under the sun's glow,
In the meadow of giggles, enjoy the flow!

Enchantment in Every Leaf

A leaf fell down and did a flip,
It landed softly on my lip.
"Excuse me!" shouted the tulip bright,
"Why's your face breeding this delight?"

The daisies giggled in a row,
As the sun began to glow.
"Be careful now, don't make a mess!"
"Of pollen soup? We confess!"

The grass was tickling everyone,
A playful dance that just begun.
A dandelion let out a snort,
"Did you hear that? We are quite short!"

They swayed and laughed without a care,
In the wild garden's joyful air.
Each leaf a joker, each bud a bard,
What a comedy, oh my dear yard!

The Garden's Brief Embrace

In the garden's arms, I tripped and fell,
Kissed by worms that cast a spell.
"Who invited you?" a rose did shout,
"This isn't a party, you're going out!"

Bees wore hats and sipped on tea,
While ants debated, 'Who's next to flee?'
"Hey you, don't look at me like that!
I'm no eavesdropper on your chit-chat!"

The tomatoes blushed, oh what a sight!
"Is it hot in here or just our plight?"
Cucumbers rolled, proud and aloof,
While carrots tried to get on the roof.

Together they formed a ruckus loud,
The funniest bunch in the leafy crowd.
A garden giggle here and a snort there,
Embraces of joy all laid bare!

The Abode of Translunar Blooms

In a garden where laughter grows,
The blooms tell stories, everyone knows.
"What's on the menu?" the sunflowers grinned,
"Last week's gossip? Or sweets that we've pinned?"

A foxglove waltzes on dainty feet,
"Are we too flowery, or just too sweet?"
Lilies twirled in a dazzling whirl,
"Let's plan a ball, I'll give it a twirl!"

The peonies puffed in splendid dress,
"Who wants to play with our floral finesse?"
"I can juggle, look!" shouted a sprig,
But dropped it all and did a big jig.

Each bloom was wild, each petal a jest,
In this house of flora, laughter's the quest.
So come join the fun, don't be so glum,
In this world of whims where blossoms hum!

Chronicles of the Bough

Under boughs that whispered tales,
A squirrel squeaked; he found some snails.
"Why run away? We're friends, I swear!
Can't you share in my zany affair?"

Branches tangled in gossip wild,
Agreeing they've all been exiled.
The woodpecker drummed with a grin,
"Let's start a band, I'll join you in!"

Leaves rustled loudly, wanting to shout,
"Who made the mess? Let's throw it out!"
A friendly breeze caught everyone's ear,
"Let's make a ruckus, sing loud and clear!"

And so they laughed, in dappled shade,
Adding humor to the leafy parade.
As each bough gleamed with childish cheer,
They stitched delight, one grin at a year!

Lament of the Blossoming Tree

Oh, how I sway and twist with glee,
But bees just laugh and flee from me.
My blooms are bright, my leaves so green,
Yet squirrels think I'm a trampoline!

A gusty wind, my branches shake,
I'd rather dance than break a flake.
But watch me try to hold my stance,
Instead, I tumble—what a prance!

The kids all giggle, pointing near,
"Look at that tree, it's full of cheer!"
But when they climb, oh what a sight,
The bark yells, "This isn't right!"

Between the squirrels and playful kids,
I'm just a tree with leafy bids.
Next spring I'll frown, but just for fun,
Let's see who else can make me run!

Threads of Nature's Tapestry

In a garden grand where colors mix,
I'm weaving blooms, my clever tricks.
A daisy says, "I'm best at pink!"
While a rose calls out, "You must rethink!"

I spun a yarn of green and gold,
But slugs believed they could be bold.
Oh nature's threads, they weave and tangle,
While butterflies just dance and dangle!

A spider claims it's all his thread,
While ants march through the colors spread.
Together we stroll, a parade so bright,
In threads of laughter from morning to night!

As petals flap and laughter rings,
We'll stitch some joy with all our flings.
A tapestry made of whimsy and cheer,
With nature's quirks, we revel here!

Colors of the Hidden Grove

In a grove where secrets lay afloat,
The trees all gossip, quite remote.
"Did you see that fox with a pink bow?"
He prances about like he's the show!

The mushrooms giggle as they sprout,
With polka dots that dance about.
"Let's have a party, bright and loud!"
They invite the clouds, feeling proud!

The flowers twirl, their colors clash,
With purple and yellow in a splash.
"Who's the fairest?" asks a shy fern,
"I can hardly wait for my turn!"

In this hidden grove, a ruckus brews,
As colors mingle with laughter and hues.
What a lovely mess, this nature's play,
Where everyone blooms in a comical way!

The Dance of the Wildflowers

The wildflowers dance, oh what a sight!
They jiggle and wiggle from morning till night.
"Let's show the daisies how we can groove!"
With bee DJs spinning, they all move!

A rabbit hops in, with a wiggly tail,
While butterflies flutter, they never fail.
"Join us!" they yell, as they take a chance,
To join the waltz in the grassy expanse!

The breeze carries tunes from a nearby brook,
While elder trees sway, all it took.
"Let's have a ball, beneath starlit skies!"
While crickets provide the sweet lullabies!

So swirl around under the moon's soft glow,
The wildflowers laugh, putting on a show.
Nature's jesters in a colorful trance,
With every petal, they twirl and prance!

Garden of Forgotten Dreams

In a garden where the weeds propose,
Gnomes dance in shoes that don't quite close.
Rabbits wear hats, a curious sight,
Chasing butterflies, they take to flight.

The sunflowers gossip, their heads held high,
As daisies spin tales of the day gone by.
Bees take a break, sipping tea in style,
While worms compete in a three-legged mile.

The carrots debate on who's the best,
Radishes laugh, their roots quite blessed.
The scarecrow's humor is rather dry,
As clouds above play at hide and fly.

So wander through this playful space,
Where flowers giggle and dance with grace.
In this whimsical patch, let's all agree,
The fun never ends, you just wait and see!

Echoes in the Flora

In the forest where the squirrels chat,
A mushroom wears a dapper hat.
Frogs croon tunes, but hit a wrong note,
While hedgehogs ponder their fashion quote.

Lizards lounge on rocks, oh so laid back,
Plotting a heist for a tasty snack.
The chirping crickets join the fake band,
As fireflies flash, like a disco planned.

Petunias flex, trying to be cool,
But pansies mock, calling them a fool.
Trees gossip low, in hushed leafy tones,
As acorns drop like uninvited drones.

Joyful echoes fill the air so sweet,
In this flora, life's a funny treat.
So join the laughter, don't be shy,
Under this canopy, let spirits fly!

Fragrance of the Serene

In the meadow where the lilies beam,
Old daisies dream, or so it seems.
Their roots are tangled, a messy art,
Yet they craft bouquets to warm the heart.

Pollen parties make quite the buzz,
As clovers dance, just because.
The roses swear they have the best scent,
While violets plot a scented event.

The sun's a joker, playing peek-a-boo,
As rabbits plot a comedic coup.
Gardens chuckle at the skies above,
Stealing rays, like laughter, from love.

In this serene land of fragrant cheer,
Fun and giggles are always near.
So take a whiff of this joyful dream,
Where flowers and laughter make quite the team!

Secrets Beneath the Canopy

Beneath the leaves, mischief unfolds,
With beetles spinning tales retold.
A chipmunk's stash is a sight to see,
As nuts roll out in a comedy spree.

The vines weave stories of a hidden past,
With raccoons laughing, their shadows cast.
Fungi plot, with a mischievous glee,
Whispering secrets to the buzzing bee.

A sloth hangs low, fashionably late,
In the soft moss, they just can't wait.
Squirrels debate whose acorn's the best,
While owls wear spectacles, taking a rest.

In this secret world of foliage and game,
Every creature laughs, yet none feels the same.
So roam through the mystery, join in the fun,
In the dappled light, life's just begun!

Symbols of the Verdant Realm

In the garden where daffodils dance,
A snail took a leap, gave fate a chance.
Worms on a picnic, what a sight to see,
Sharing their sandwiches, just them and a bee.

The flowers all giggle, whispering cheer,
As a squirrel in a suit drinks its root beer.
A rabbit in shades reads the news of the day,
While daisies debate who will lead the ballet.

A hedgehog in slippers finds joy in the dirt,
With berries and herbs, he's flexing his shirt.
The mushrooms sing loudly, "Join in the jest!"
While ants in a conga line giggle and rest.

So wander this land of delights and of cheer,
Where every small creature is wild with good cheer.
In this world so bright, where fun takes the stage,
Even the grasshoppers dance with great rage.

Petal Dreams in the Twilight

As night falls, the crickets throw rave,
While moonflowers giggle, a club for the brave.
Fireflies twinkle like bubbles of light,
While owls crack jokes at the bugs in their flight.

A raccoon with flair dons a sparkly hat,
Stealing some snacks, he won't get caught flat.
The trees sway their branches, all dancing in line,
While frogs leap in rhythm, all feeling divine.

The clouds wear pajamas, floating on high,
The stars bet on who's the best dancer—oh my!
The dark is a canvas, for laughter and cheer,
With each little creature, the vibe stays sincere.

Tomorrow we'll wake, and the fun will restart,
In twilight's warm glow, nature plays every part.
So join in the revel, with smiles all around,
For laughter and joy in this place will abound.

Colors of Awakening

Morning breaks with a peep from the sun,
A rooster sings loudly—thinks he's the one.
The tulips are gossiping, stand tall with pride,
While daisies nod along, enjoying the ride.

A butterfly stumbles, trips over a leaf,
It's hard being graceful, causing much grief.
But laughter erupts from the blossoms so fair,
As the wind swoops in, tousling their hair.

Frogs leap in puddles, splashing with glee,
They've formed a conga line—what a sight to see!
While ladybugs giggle, in polka-dot suits,
As they dance with the bees in their snappy old boots.

So come to this canvas, where colors run free,
And join in the jest, it's all meant to be.
In this merry domain, where the sun calls the tune,
We celebrate nature—join in, it's afternoon!

The Hushed Voice of Nature

In the hush of the woods, where silence can sing,
A rabbit makes plans for a wild spring fling.
Mice whisper secrets while hiding from cats,
And turtles discuss who's the fastest of fats.

A squirrel with charm breaks into a jig,
Showing off moves while he's outsmarting a fig.
The leaves rustle softly, "Did you hear the news?
The grass is wearing shoes and the sky's painted blues!"

As dawn paints the world with a brush made of gold,
The flowers debate who's the bravest and bold.
The wind carries laughter, a symphony sweet,
While all of creation finds joy in the beat.

So listen, and giggle, at nature's grand show,
Where creatures unite in a frolicsome flow.
In this hushed harmony, the fun is alive,
In the whispers of nature, we all get to thrive.

Pathways of Sunlit Splendor

Bumblebees buzzing, oh what a sight,
In their tiny buzz suits, they dance with delight.
Sunflowers giggle as they bow to the sun,
Beneath the warm rays, they all have their fun.

Worms in the dirt discuss gardening tricks,
While daisies share gossip about new fashion picks.
The grasshoppers leap, dressed to impress,
Holding a contest for the best-legged dress!

The ladybugs laugh, they're the judges today,
They tally up scores as they fumble and sway.
Count your colors and spots, don't be too shy,
In this flower-filled kingdom where dreams touch the sky!

A butterfly floats, it's quite the parade,
With sparkles and glam, all nature's charade.
They twirl and they swirl, the whole garden's a stage,
A comical tale where laughter won't age!

Dreams Cradled by Greenery

Under leafy blankets, thoughts start to sprout,
Ants in a conga line, shrieking about.
They're planning a feast with crumbs so divine,
A picnic for critters, everyone's fine!

The frogs in the pond croak a topsy tune,
While squirrels play tag under the light of the moon.
Their acorns are treasures, for laughs and for foes,
What in the world, do they wear on their toes?

Bunnies are plotting a fashion showcase,
With carrots for hats, they'll light up the place!
Even hedgehogs join in, with spikes all a-glow,
At this whimsical gala, the laughs just won't slow.

From petals to hedges, with humor sincere,
Nature's a circus, come gather near.
With dreams running wild, and glee in the air,
Join us, dear friends, if you dare!

A Haven for the Soul

In a nook of the woods, where sunshine beams bright,
Twirling mushrooms giggle, what a funny sight!
They share silly stories from long, long ago,
While a grouchy old stump grumbles soft "oh no!"

Chirping crickets sing a jolly refrain,
Every note a tickle, a delightful strain.
They host an orchestra of bugs on the grass,
While butterflies yawn — oh, the time they let pass!

A turtle crawls slowly, yet he claims he is fast,
He's challenging snails, but not coming in last!
With hats made of clover, they race for the prize,
A plate full of leaves, oh, what a surprise!

Laughter rings out in this cozy retreat,
Each creature finds joy in the life that's sweet.
In this haven of whimsy, where silly dreams dwell,
Find a spark in your spirit, and laugh with us well!

Whispers of Blossoms

The tulips confide in the breezy blow,
Their whispers of secrets, only the wind knows.
With petals that giggle in colors so bright,
They throw a grand party, fueled by delight!

Dandelions puff as they scatter their dreams,
While squirrels trade jokes by the babbling streams.
Their antics are wild, a comedic delight,
As they tumble and fumble in nature's pure light.

The violets play pranks, hiding under the grass,
While crickets do stand-up, the audience laughs!
The forest is chuckling at each little jest,
With laughter that echoes, it's truly the best.

In the heart of this garden, joy freely flows,
With giggles and glee, every creature now knows.
Embrace the humor, let your spirit ignite,
For this world of bright blooms is a purest delight!

In the Heart of Wilds

A squirrel danced with a curious hat,
Chasing shadows of a lazy cat.
Bees took selfies, buzzing with glee,
While flowers giggled, 'Look at me!'

A frog recited his epic tale,
But ended up caught in a wet veil.
The trees whispered secrets, kind of absurd,
As the wind played tag with a flapping bird.

Mice held a party beneath the moon,
Served cheese and crackers, a quirky boon.
The owls hooted, adding their flair,
While stars blinked down, with knowing stare.

In the heart of wilds, life is a jest,
With laughter echoing, it's truly blessed.
So stomp your feet and join the show,
Where the world is wacky, and joy will flow!

The Serenity of Unfurling

A daisy dressed up in polka dots,
Declared it a gala, inviting the bots.
With sunflowers swaying, and roses in tow,
They twirled and twirled, putting on a show.

The wind brought gossip from blossoms afar,
As butterflies danced beneath neon stars.
They slipped on their shades, saying, 'Look who's here!'
A cactus in sneakers, spreading the cheer.

A geranium whispered, 'Let's sing a tune!'
So they all harmonized under the moon.
With bees as the band humming sweet thrum,
While ants were the dancers, all wiggly and plumb.

In this wild garden, life takes flight,
With silliness blooming both day and night.
So join the fun, don't be at a loss,
In the serenity of unfurling, we're the boss!

Echoes of Forgotten Gardens

In a garden once grand, now lost in a haze,
A gnome was discovered, in a curious phase.
He'd mislaid his hat, looking quite dire,
While the hedgehogs chuckled, alive with desire.

The rhubarb stretched, saying, 'Look at me!'
While kale plotted ways to break free.
A daffodil laughed at a passing weed,
'You're just a wannabe, but that's not the creed!'

Tomatoes held meetings, discussing their plight,
Overripe and splattered, a sad, funny sight.
They planned a revolt against the chef's spoon,
With dreams of freedom beneath the pale moon.

In forgotten gardens, joy reigns supreme,
Where veggies and flowers plot with a dream.
So pull up a chair, let the laughter erupt,
In this wild green chaos, we're perfectly corrupt!

Tranquil Reveries on Soft Earth

On soft earthen beds where fungi grow,
The mushrooms threw parties with an oaky glow.
They donned tiny hats, oh what a sight,
While snails in tuxedos slid in with delight.

The daisies debated the best kind of sun,
While worms played chess, having so much fun.
A wise old oak barked jokes from high,
With laughter so hearty, it reached for the sky.

In shadows of crickets, night took a peek,
With moonbeams chuckling at what they seek.
Glow-worms lit pathways, twinkling and bright,
While frogs croaked sonnets, embracing the night.

Tranquil reveries, where silliness thrives,
In a world of whimsy, where each heart arrives.
Join this delight, let your worries unearth,
In the gentle embrace of soft, silly earth!

Echoes of Nature's Palette

In the garden where gnomes play,
Colors dance in bright ballet.
Butterflies wear their finest clothes,
While the worms grumble 'bout their toes.

Ladybugs have a picnic feast,
Ants march in like a perfect beast.
The daisies gossip, oh so loud,
While the sunflowers attract a crowd.

Bees buzzing tunes of sweet delight,
In their hive, they argue who's right.
Roses blush and roll their eyes,
As violets taunt with sweet goodbyes.

In this chaos of color and cheer,
Nature's giggles fill the atmosphere.
With each bloom, life's jest expands,
A world alive with funny hands.

Veils of Soft Color

The tulips wear their frilly gowns,
While the daisies sport paper crowns.
A butterfly lost his way to brunch,
And the lilies laugh, giving him a punch.

Zinnias throw a vibrant rave,
While petals sway along the wave.
Joking with the wind, they twirl,
All while the wise old oak just curls.

Sunflowers wink with golden tones,
As bees buzz like they're on phones.
The hydrangeas tease with hues,
Whispering secrets to amused blues.

In this garden of painted glee,
Every root and stem wants to be free!
With laughter bright amidst the blooms,
Life's a party, bursting with booms!

Blooms of the Divine

A rose tries to outshine the sun,
While the daisies giggle, having fun.
The peonies put on a grand show,
Claiming the garden's their type of flow.

Violets plot a prank on the oak,
While the sage offers up a joke.
A fragrant breeze catches the scene,
Spreading laughter, herb and green.

Tulips tease the frogs on their log,
"Ribbit loud; let's start a blog!"
The garden's a stage of comic delights,
Where petals dance under the lights.

Each bud is a performer, vibrant and bold,
With connections that can't be sold.
In this rosy, laughing sphere,
Nature's smile is ever near.

Harmony in the Hedges

In the thicket, hedges collide,
With bees buzzing, full of pride.
A squirrel juggles acorns with flair,
While the ferns snicker, full of air.

A dandelion believes it's a star,
Claiming its roots are never far.
With a puff, it shouts, "I'm the one!"
While violets snicker, "Oh, what fun!"

The hedges wave like old jazz bands,
Shaking in rhythm, no idle hands.
Twirling petals, a fanciful sight,
As they dance together, day and night.

Here in the hedges, laughter grows,
In this wild garden, anything goes!
With every leaf, a chuckle flows,
Nature crafts the funniest shows.

Fragments of Morning Dew

Morning drops like silly clowns,
Swinging from the leaves like frowns.
They giggle round with cheeky cheer,
Wishing for a cup of beer.

The sun flips pancakes in the sky,
While flowers dance, oh my, oh my!
They sway and twirl in joyous spree,
As bees hum tunes of comedy.

Each whisper and rustle a little prank,
The breeze just plays, oh what a rank!
They tease the grass in goofy lays,
As laughter blooms through sunny rays.

So sprinkle laughter in your brew,
And join the dance of morning dew.
For in this garden, wild and free,
Life's just a laugh, come taste the glee!

The Language of the Foliage

The leaves all gossip in a breeze,
Cackling jokes like blooming teas.
They speak in whispers, cheeky tunes,
Making trouble with soft baboons.

Branches wave, a quirky crew,
Squirrels chuckle, "What's it to you?"
Their chatter rolls, it fluffs the air,
Telling tales of life so rare.

Each rustle spins a tale so fine,
Like nature's sitcom, purely divine.
They poke fun at the wandering snail,
Who wears its shell like a shiny veil.

In this realm where laughter grows,
Foliage thrives on funny prose.
Join in the laughter, let it flow,
For nature's jest is the best show!

Hues of a Forgotten Paradise

Colors blend in a joyful fight,
Painting flowers day and night.
With laughter spills from pots of dew,
Creating smiles, a vibrant view.

The daisies claim they're best at dance,
While tulips wink, they take a chance.
"Let's color this garden with silly flair,
And fill it with giggles beyond compare!"

Butterflies tease with a colorful spin,
Chasing their tails with a cheeky grin.
The hues collide in a vivid mess,
Just like a painter in sheer distress.

So grasp your brush and join the fun,
In the hues where laughter's spun.
For in this chaos, wild and gay,
Lies the heart of a bright bouquet!

The Soft Murmur of Leaves

Leaves whisper secrets, oh what a tease,
Tickling the air with flirtatious ease.
They wiggle and dance in the soft twilight,
Echoing jokes in the fading light.

A leaf makes faces, a nutty laugh,
Bemoaning the tree's "crazy hair 'n' calf!"
With chuckles rolling from branch to bark,
Their humor shines like a firefly spark.

In shadows deep, the pranks arise,
As nature's jesters wear quirky ties.
So listen close, to their witty banter,
For in their words, there's always a canter.

Join the fun with the fluttering sound,
Where laughter and leaves are tightly bound.
In this realm of silly delight,
Nature's whispers bring joy to the night!

The Lure of Fragrant Paths

In gardens where the flowers wink,
A bee will pause, just to rethink.
He thinks of nectar, sweet and bright,
But gets distracted by a kite.

The daisies giggle in the breeze,
While busy ants jog with such ease.
They wear their tiny workday frowns,
As butterflies just float around.

A blooming fool would take a dare,
And dance with carrots, unaware.
The radish makes a cheeky joke,
While glancing at the spinach cloak.

So roam the paths where petals play,
With scents that tease in bright array.
Just heed the laughter on the way,
And let the funny flowers sway.

Eden's Gentle Breath

The lilies laugh, they've heard a pun,
They joke about their leafy run.
A squirrel slips on morning dew,
And spills his acorns, just a few.

The sunbeams tickle every sprout,
While giggling vines peek in and out.
A hedgehog rolls, trying to hide,
But spikes can't stop the joyful ride.

Sweet breezes tease the bumblebees,
As daisies sway with courage, please!
Each blossom wears a silly grin,
And plays a game of peek-a-boo win.

So stroll through laughter, oh so light,
Where nature spins in pure delight.
Each breath is filled with chirps and cheer,
In this sweet sanctuary where we steer.

Within the Leafy Haven

In leafy nooks, the creatures dwell,
A snail narrates, but who can tell?
His friends just laugh, they find it grand,
As butterflies discuss the land.

The mossy carpet's soft and green,
Where tiny fairies flip and preen.
They share a joke about a seed,
And giggle loud, oh yes indeed!

The choosy buds refuse to bloom,
Insisting on a fancy room.
They all debate on which's the best,
While sitting cozily, quite at rest.

So wander through this happy place,
With laughter swirling in the space.
Each giggle floats on fragrant air,
In this haven of joy, we'll share.

The Allure of Wild Blooms

The wild blooms dance in sunny rays,
Their colors mix in joyful ways.
A bumblebee just took a chance,
And got caught in a daisy dance.

The ladybugs wear polka dots,
And gossip 'bout the sun's hot shots.
A clever frog croaks out a tune,
While hiding from the afternoon.

The thorns debate with blooms so bright,
Who gets the sun and who takes flight?
While rascally vines do twirl and climb,
In nature's rhythm, oh so prime.

So join the laughter in the fields,
Where every flower joyfully yields.
With every petal, every cheer,
You'll find the fun is always near.

Serenity in each Bloom

In the garden, bees loudly hum,
Flowers dance, shaking their bum.
A squirrel in shades, styling so slick,
Who knew nature could be such a trick?

Pansies giggle under the sun,
While daisies say, let's have some fun!
Tulips gossip with vibrant flair,
"Who wore it better?" It's too debonair!

Breezes chuckle, tickling the grass,
As butterflies flit, feeling quite brash.
It's a riot, this colorful spree,
Who knew plants had such comedy?

In this patch, laughter reigns true,
Nature's jesters in every hue.
So here's to blooms, with a wink and a laugh,
Join the joke, let's dance on their path!

A Symphony of Petal Rain

Raindrops plink like a cheerful tune,
As flowers sway, they dance with the moon.
Lily pads slide, with a splish and a splash,
While frogs serenade in a joyful clash!

A quirky robin sings off-key,
While daisies sway, as proud as can be.
The sun peeks out, with a golden grin,
Even the shadows want to join in!

The ants on parade march to the beat,
Carrying crumbs for a picnic treat.
Bumbling bugs join the vibrant display,
In this silly parade, they happily play!

So let's raise a glass to this floral delight,
Where laughter and nature take flight.
For in this garden, the humor is grand,
A symphony of joy, so perfectly planned!

The Tender Leaf's Embrace

A leaf fell down, with a flump and a thud,
Landing on a snail, oh how it was chudd!
"Excuse me, dear leaf, you're blocking my way!"
The snail sighed gently, just wanted to sway.

Sunflowers stretching, with towering pride,
While the daisies giggle, and often subside.
A hedgehog in shades takes a break in the shade,
Sipping on dew, planning his parade!

This leaf takes a moment, to chat with a bud,
"Life's but a toss, like a splash in the mud!"
The flowers all laughed at their leafy friend,
Who knew a good chat could never offend?

So here's to the leaf, in its tender embrace,
Bringing joy and laughter to this lively place.
In the heart of the garden, where all critters roam,
Every leaf tells a story, every bloom finds a home!

Echoes of the Midnight Garden

When the moon glows bright in the fabric of night,
Crickets start chirping, oh what a sight!
A raccoon in pajamas roams with a snack,
While fireflies twinkle, lighting the track.

The roses whisper secrets, smelling of cheer,
As night blooms gather, their laughter sincere.
A hedgehog named Harold shares wild bedtime tales,
Of epic adventures down mystical trails!

Bats swoop and dive, with laughter in flight,
As the stars wink back, in sheer delight.
The flowers hold hands, in a night-time pact,
Whispering dreams, oh what fun is this act!

In this midnight garden, where giggles abound,
The magic of nature dances all around.
So let's join this laughter, let's laugh and let be,
In the echoes of night, we're all wild and free!

The Realm of Flowering Spirits

In a garden where daisies gleam,
A bee danced in a wild daydream.
He tripped on a rose, said, "Oh dear!"
Now he's buzzing without any fear.

The petals giggle, in colors bright,
A daffodil sings with all its might.
"I'm the star of this floral show!"
But a weed popped up, said, "Not so slow!"

With sunflowers aiming their heads up high,
A dandelion whispered, "Oh, give it a try!"
"I can blow you away, my fluffy friend!"
The flowers chuckled, their laughter won't end.

So gather round in this blooming spree,
With humor that's sweet, as sweet as can be.
For in this realm where spirits sway,
Every leaf has a joke, come join the play!

Quietude in the Shade

Under the boughs where shadows play,
A cucumber vine tried to steal the day.
"I'm a veggie, but I'll bloom like a flower!"
Said the melon with all of its power.

While lily pads floated, so calm and cool,
A frog croak-laughed, played the jester's fool.
He hopped on a leaf, said, "What's the rush?"
"I've got time to spare, so let's take a hush!"

An ant marched by with a pile on its back,
Whispered to a snail, "What's up with my snack?"
"You're a little too fast, but I'll keep the pace!"
The snail winked, slow-moving through space.

In this quiet spot, where giggles convene,
Nature's humor paints everything green.
So relax in the shade, let laughter unfold,
In the whispers of leaves, there's magic untold.

Whispers Among the Tulips

The tulips are chatting, what a sight to see,
One said, "Do you think this wind likes me?"
It swayed and twirled, a playful dance,
But tripped on a daisy, oh what a chance!

A lilac peeped in, full of delight,
"This bouquet party is quite out of sight!"
The violets nodded, with smirks on their faces,
As petals jumped into flower-filled races.

A bumblebee buzzed, full of sass and cheer,
"With me around, you've nothing to fear!"
But tangled up in tulips, he started to sway,
"Help! I think I've lost my way!"

Amidst all the laughter, the sun shines so bright,
In this floral fiesta, everything feels right.
So join in the fun with petals so bold,
For humor in blooms is a story retold!

The Tranquil Spectrum

In a spectrum of colors, so vibrant and free,
A rainbow named Larry claimed, "Look at me!"
But the violets giggled, leaning one way,
"You've hardly got shades—give it a day!"

The orange marigolds danced in a whirl,
While sunflowers shouted, "Let's give it a twirl!"
A peony blushed, but the daffodils roared,
"Come get your groove on, let's strike a chord!"

In this tranquil abode, where laughter is loud,
The spectrum spread joy to both humble and proud.
"A kaleidoscope joke?" asked the rose with a tease,
"Only if it's funny; we aim to please!"

So, let's paint the garden with chuckles and glee,
For every bloom has a spirit so free.
In this riot of colors, you'll surely find cheer,
And the joke of the garden will always be near.

Whispers of Blossoms

In the garden, seeds hold chats,
With daisies discussing hats.
Roses giggle at the sight,
While sunflowers dance with delight.

Bees buzzing, always late,
Claim they just had a dinner date.
Tulips tease with their colors bright,
And lilies laugh at their own height.

Worms wiggling, a secret club,
Throwing parties, joined by a shrub.
Petunias join in, what a scene,
Dancing under the leafy green.

With every rustle, we can hear,
Plants sharing gossip, oh so dear.
In this realm where laughter grows,
Nature's mirth, everyone knows!

Lush Secrets of the Grove

In the grove where shadows play,
Trees trade secrets, night and day.
Acorns plot to roll downhill,
While branches argue, who's the chill?

Squirrels taking bets on rain,
Claiming they'll outsmart the pain.
Flowers gossip, what's the trend?
Will the violets soon amend?

Fluttering leaves join the fun,
With whispers shared on the run.
Roots entwined in silly schemes,
Nature giggles as it dreams.

In this lush and lively scene,
Every critter wears a grin.
Grove of joy, it never ends,
Where laughter blooms and nature bends!

Radiance Awakens

Morning light brings winks of joy,
Bees buzzin' like a toy.
Sunshine tickles every petal,
While shadows try to find a medal.

Morning glories yawn and stretch,
Caffeine from dew is their fetch.
Daffodils flex in a row,
Saying, 'Look at us, stealing the show!'

Birds chirp loudly, a happy song,
But the bushes whisper, 'They're wrong.'
Nestled mice with tales to tell,
Giggle while giving their nightly bell.

In dawn's embrace, the world awakes,
With each smile a ripple makes.
Joy unfolds in every hue,
Radiance sparkles, so should you!

Tapestry of Flora

In a patchwork of colors bright,
Plants weave tales from day to night.
Hydrangeas in gossip rings around,
While sunflowers make the funniest sounds.

Mulch chuckles at the soil's jest,
And roots share stories, doing their best.
A dandelion with a complex plan,
To become a wish for every man.

Lavender spins tales of calm,
While violets offer the sweetest balm.
Lily pads float, keeping it cool,
Claiming the pond's their exclusive pool.

With whispers carried on the breeze,
Nature laughs, aiming to please.
In this lush tapestry of fun,
Every bloom is a joyous pun!

www.ingramcontent.com/pod-product-compliance
Lightning Source LLC
Chambersburg PA
CBHW071824160426
43209CB00003B/197